Dedicated to my wife Rebecca, daughter Mary Ashleigh, and son Matthew whom I love dearly. But first and foremost, I dedicate this to my Lord and Savior, Jesus, to whom my faith lies.

Contents

Chapter 1: Introduction

This is the first book of a five-part series that discusses what it means to be walking a life as a Christian; that is, it helps the reader to understand the meaning of walking a life of Christ who set an example for us so many years ago which is evidenced in not only the teachings of the Gospels and other books of the New Testament but also prefaced by writings in the books of the Old Testament (known by Jews as the *Tanakh*) such as in the Book of Isaiah which are read by both the Jewish and Christian people of the world. Walking a life of Christ includes following principles such as love, compassion, forgiveness, humility, and service to others. Walking a life of Christ involves not only believing in Jesus as the Son of God but also striving to emulate his character and actions in daily life. It often entails practicing virtues such as honesty, integrity, kindness, and selflessness, and seeking to live in harmony with God's will as revealed through Jesus's teachings. It's essentially about adopting a lifestyle guided by Christian values and principles.

This first book approaches one of the aspects of walking a life of Christ: walking in faith. Specifically in Christianity, walking in faith involves trusting in God's promises, relying on His guidance, and believing in the teachings of Jesus Christ. It means having confidence in God's goodness, wisdom, and sovereignty, even in the face of uncertainty or adversity.

Walking in faith requires a deep conviction that God is present and actively involved in one's life, even when circumstances may seem challenging or difficult to understand. It involves surrendering control and placing one's trust in God's plan, knowing that He is ultimately in control of all things.

Practically, walking in faith involves living out one's beliefs in daily life, making decisions based on spiritual principles, and relying on prayer and meditation for guidance and strength. It often entails stepping out of one's comfort zone, taking risks, and embracing uncertainty with the belief that God will provide and guide accordingly.

Overall, walking in faith is a journey of trust, obedience, and reliance on a higher power, with the understanding that faith can sustain and empower individuals through life's various trials and triumphs.

~~~~~~~~~~~~~~~~~~~~~~~~~~~~~~~~~~~~~~

Personal Testimony: *In the summer of 2014, I was unemployed for a few months and my 17-year-old son asked me, "How can you be sure that God will provide you a job?" I told him, "Because I have faith that God will provide". Within a few weeks, I received a phone call from a government contractor wanting me to come in for an interview. I told the recruiter that I did not apply for this job and asked how they found my name. The recruiter told me that they found me online. I knew at this very moment that God had answered my prayer and my faith in Him. The evening after my interview, I was called back and hired. God is good all the time!*
~~~~~~~~~~~~~~~~~~~~~~~~~~~~~~~~~~~~~~

Prayer:

Dear heavenly Father, I pray that the readers of this book and the ensuing series are blessed beyond measure by your Son and our Lord and Savior Jesus Christ to whom all things are possible. I also pray that you guide these readers and help them understand what it means to walk a life of Christ and understand that it is not only for their spiritual growth but that this walk helps them provide an example and beacon of hope and strength to others. I thank you Lord for giving me the words and guidance to put together this book and the ensuing series and I pray that they touch many hearts and help bring others to you. I ask all of this in Jesus's name, Amen.

Chapter 2: Trusting in God and Finding Confidence in Him

"Trust in the Lord with all your heart and lean not on your own understanding; in all your ways submit to him, and he will make your paths straight." - **Proverbs 3:5-6 (NIV)**

To trust in God and find confidence in Him means to rely completely on His character, His promises, and His guidance in every aspect of life. It involves surrendering one's plans, desires, and worries to God, believing that He is faithful and capable of fulfilling His promises.

Trusting in God means having faith that He is all-powerful, all-knowing, and ever-present and that His plans are ultimately for our good, even if we may not understand them now. It involves placing our confidence in His wisdom, goodness, and love, *regardless of the circumstances we face.*

Finding confidence in God means recognizing that our worth and security come from Him alone, not from our achievements or circumstances. It involves resting in the assurance that we are deeply loved and cared for by our Heavenly Father, and that He is always with us, providing strength, comfort, and guidance through life's challenges.

Ultimately, trusting in God and finding confidence in Him is a transformative act of faith that brings peace, security, and hope, enabling us to face life's uncertainties with courage and resilience. It is a continual journey of deepening our relationship with God and learning to rely more fully on His grace and provision.

Let's look at a few Bible passages (taken from the NIV) that specifically deal with this aspect of trust and confidence and delve into a deeper understanding by dissecting each passage into parts.

Proverbs 3:5-6

"Trust in the Lord with all your heart and lean not on your own understanding; in all your ways submit to him, and he will make your paths straight."

Proverbs 3:5-6 is often considered a profound statement of faith and a call to live in obedience and reliance on God's guidance. It emphasizes the importance of trusting God wholeheartedly, acknowledging His wisdom above human understanding, and submitting to His direction in all aspects of life. The promise of straight paths suggests a life guided by God's wisdom and aligned with His will.

"Trust in the Lord with all your heart" – emphasizes the importance of having complete trust in God which is better defined as a wholehearted reliance on the Lord. This further indicates a deep and unwavering confidence in His wisdom and guidance.

"…and lean not on your own understanding;" – in the big picture of things, we have a very limited perspective which also may be somewhat biased at times. We should not depend on this limited perspective; what this verse is telling us is to acknowledge God's wisdom and sovereignty in all matters.

"…in all your ways submit to him," – this verse encourages acknowledging God's authority and seeking His guidance in **EVERY** aspect of life, not just in specific areas or areas convenient to us.

"…and he will make your paths straight." – this again follows the call to trust and submit. If you acknowledge His wisdom and see His guidance, He will direct and guide your path in a way that aligns with His purposes.

Jeremiah 17:7

"But blessed is the one who trusts in the Lord, whose confidence is in him."

Jeremiah 17:7 echoes a theme found throughout the Bible, particularly in the Psalms and Proverbs, highlighting the positive outcomes of trusting in the Lord. It conveys the idea that those who place their confidence in God experience a state of blessedness, regardless of external circumstances. This verse encourages believers to cultivate a trust-filled relationship with God, finding security and joy in relying on His unfailing character and guidance.

"Blessed is the one who trusts in the Lord," – this is a declaration of blessing for those who place their trust in the Lord. Those who place their trust in Lord signify a state of happiness, well-being, and divine favor.

"…whose confidence is in him." – blessedness is tied to the individual's confidence in the Lord. Trust and confidence in God go hand in hand,

emphasizing a deep and unwavering reliance on His faithfulness and promises.

Habakkuk 2:4

"See, the enemy is puffed up; his desires are not upright – but the righteous person will live by his faithfulness."

Habakkuk 2:4 is a significant verse that has had a profound impact on biblical theology. The New Testament quotes this verse several times, emphasizing the concept of justification by faith. The apostle Paul references it in Romans 1:17 and Galatians 3:11, highlighting that righteousness comes not through adherence to the law but through faith in God.

In the context of Habakkuk, the verse likely speaks to the idea that those who are considered righteous in God's eyes are characterized by their faithfulness and trust in God, rather than relying on their achievements or the trappings of worldly success. It sets the stage for a theological understanding that righteousness is imputed by faith rather than earned through human works.

"See, the enemy is puffed up; his desires are not upright –" – those who oppose God are usually expressing arrogance and wickedness through pride and immoral desires.

"…but the righteous person will live by his faithfulness." – encapsulates the idea that righteousness is not merely about adherence to rules or rituals but about a deep, abiding trust in God that permeates every aspect of life. It's about living in a way that demonstrates reliance

on God's faithfulness and aligns with His character and purposes. It is important to note that worldly success does not necessarily indicate one who is righteous in God's eyes.

Hebrews 11:1

"Now faith is confidence in what we hope for and assurance about what we do not see."

Hebrews 11:1 emphasizes that faith is not blind or unfounded; instead, it is a grounded confidence and assurance in the promises of God, even when those promises may not be immediately visible or tangible. This verse serves as a foundational statement on the nature of faith, setting the stage for the examples of faith that follow in Hebrews 11, often referred to as the "faith hall of fame" or the "heroes of faith" chapter.

"Now faith is confidence in what we hope for" – this goes beyond mere belief; it is a conviction and confidence in the certainty of what God has promised.

"…assurance about what we do not see." – this is not based on physical evidence but on a profound certainty in the existence of spiritual realities and God's faithfulness to His Word.

Overall, trusting in God and finding confidence in Him is a transformative act of faith that involves relying on His character, believing in His promises, surrendering control, finding security and peace, and acting with boldness and courage under His will.

Meditation: in the spaces provided write down your thoughts and responses to these verses and summarize what trusting in God and finding confidence in Him means to you.

Chapter 3: Faith as an Antidote to Fear, Anxiety, and Life's Challenges

"He replied, 'You of little faith, why are you so afraid?' Then he got up and rebuked the winds and the waves, and it was completely calm." **- Matthew 8:26**

Faith can indeed serve as an antidote to fear and anxiety in various ways:

Trust in a Higher Power: Faith often involves trusting in a higher power or divine being, which can provide a sense of comfort and security, knowing that one is not alone in facing challenges.

Belief in Divine Providence: Many religious traditions teach that everything happens for a reason and that there is a greater purpose or plan at work in the universe. This belief can help individuals cope with uncertainty and adversity, knowing that their lives are ultimately in the hands of a loving and compassionate deity.

Spiritual Practices: Engaging in spiritual practices such as prayer, meditation, and worship can promote a sense of calmness and inner peace, helping to alleviate feelings of anxiety and worry.

Community Support: Faith communities often provide a strong support network where individuals can find encouragement, solidarity, and practical assistance in times of need. Being part of a community that shares common beliefs and values can help alleviate feelings of isolation and loneliness.

Hope and Resilience: Faith can instill a sense of hope and optimism, reminding individuals that even in the darkest of times, there is always the possibility of redemption, healing, and renewal. This sense of hope can bolster resilience and help individuals navigate through life's challenges with courage and perseverance.

Overall, faith offers a source of strength, comfort, and hope that can help individuals confront their fears and anxieties with greater resilience and inner peace.

Here are some verses that directly address how faith becomes a barrier against fear, anxiety, and adversity:

Psalm 28:7

"The LORD is my strength and my shield; my heart trusts in him, and he helps me. My heart leaps for joy, and with my song I praise him."

Psalm 28:7 is a beautiful expression of confidence and praise in God as the ultimate source of strength, protection, and assistance. It conveys a deep personal relationship with God where trust leads to joy and worship. This verse has resonated with many believers as they find encouragement and inspiration in acknowledging God's role as their strength and shield. This passage expresses praise and trust in God amid challenging circumstances.

"The LORD is my strength and shield;" – He is both the sustainer of a believer's inner strength

and the shield that guards against external threats.

"…my heart trusts in him; and he helps me." – the heart relies on God's faithfulness and God responds to this trust by providing assistance and support.

"My heart leaps for joy," – a profound and emotional response to God's intervention.

"…and with my song I praise him." – indicates a joyful and celebratory response to God's goodness and help. What is important to remember here is that praise and song should not just be a response to good things that happen in your life. Just remember the story as told in Acts 16:25-26:

"About midnight Paul and Silas were praying and singing hymns to God, and the other prisoners were listening to them. Suddenly there was such a violent earthquake that the foundations of the prison were shaken. At once all the prison doors flew open, and everyone's chains came loose."

This passage recounts the scene where Paul and Silas, who were imprisoned for their preaching, were praying and singing hymns to God despite their difficult circumstances. Their worship was noticed by the other prisoners. Then, a miraculous earthquake occurred, shaking the prison, and causing the doors to open and the prisoners' chains to be loosened. This event illustrates the power of faith and worship **even during trials**, as well as God's ability to bring about deliverance in unexpected ways.

Psalm 56:3-4

"When I am afraid, I put my trust in you. In God, whose word I praise — in God, I trust and am not afraid. What can mere mortals do to me?"

Psalm 56:3-4 reflects a profound connection between trust in God and the alleviation of fear. It emphasizes the choice to trust in God's word and character as a source of strength and confidence, even in the face of challenging circumstances. The verses inspire believers to turn to God in times of fear, finding assurance and security in Him.

"When I am afraid, I put my trust in you." — although we may have fear due to our sinful

nature, we must make a deliberate choice to place trust in God during times of anxiety. Trust must become the optimal response to fear.

"In God, whose word I praise –" – trust is rooted in a belief in the power and truth of God's spoken word which indicates confidence in the reliability and faithfulness of God's promises.

"…in God, I trust and am not afraid." – this serves as an antidote to fear. Having confidence in God's reliability overcomes fear.

"What can mere mortals do to me?" – the threats and actions of human beings are ultimately limited and powerless in comparison to the trustworthiness of God.

Philippians 4:6-7

"Do not be anxious about anything, but in every situation, by prayer and petition, with thanksgiving, present your requests to God. And the peace of God, which transcends all understanding, will guard your hearts and your minds in Christ Jesus."

This verse encourages believers to cast their anxieties upon God through prayer and thanksgiving, trusting in His provision and care. It promises that as we surrender our worries to God, His peace, which surpasses human understanding, will guard our hearts and minds. This verse highlights the power of faith and prayer in overcoming anxiety and finding inner peace during life's challenges.

"Do not be anxious about anything," – this passage begins with a clear directive to avoid anxiety. It

acknowledges the tendency for humans to worry about various aspects of life, such as health, finances, relationships, or the future. However, the instruction here is to resist succumbing to anxiety.

"…but in every situation, by prayer and petition, with thanksgiving, present your requests to God." - instead of allowing anxiety to consume us, we are encouraged to turn to God in prayer. This involves bringing our concerns, worries, and requests to Him. The passage emphasizes that prayer should be accompanied by thanksgiving, indicating an attitude of gratitude even amidst difficult circumstances.

"And the peace of God, which transcends all understanding, will guard your hearts and your minds in Christ Jesus." - the promise follows the

act of prayer and thanksgiving. It assures believers that God's peace, which surpasses human comprehension or explanation, will envelop them. This peace is described as a guardian, protecting their hearts and minds from the turmoil of anxiety and providing a sense of calm and assurance.

Overall, while faith and fear may seem opposed, they are intertwined aspects of the human experience. How individuals navigate the relationship between faith and fear often depends on their beliefs, experiences, and worldviews. Whether through overcoming fear with faith, embracing faith despite fear, or transforming fear through faith, the interplay between these two elements can profoundly shape individuals' lives and spiritual journeys.

Meditation: in the spaces provided write down your thoughts and responses to these verses and summarize how faith can help you overcome your fears, anxieties, and life's challenges.

____

____

____

____

____

____

____

____

____

____

Chapter 4: Faith as the Catalyst Toward a Personal Relationship with the Lord

"For God so loved the world that he gave his one and only Son, that whoever believes in him shall not perish but have eternal life." – **John 3:16**

Faith catalyzes a personal relationship with God by bridging the gap between humanity and the divine. Here's an overview of how faith facilitates this relationship:

Initiating Connection: Faith is the initial step towards establishing a relationship with God. It involves belief in the existence of a higher power and a willingness to engage with that power on a personal level.

Trust and Surrender: Faith entails trust and surrender to God's will and purposes. It involves acknowledging God's sovereignty and entrusting one's life and concerns to His care.

Seeking and Searching: Faith prompts individuals to seek after God, to inquire about His nature, and to pursue a deeper understanding of His character and ways. This seeking attitude fosters intimacy and closeness with God.

Communication and Prayer: Faith encourages open communication with God through prayer and meditation. It involves sharing one's thoughts, feelings, desires, and concerns with God, and being receptive to His guidance, comfort, and presence.

Obeying and Following: Genuine faith leads to obedience and a desire to follow God's commandments and teachings. It motivates individuals to align their lives with God's will and to live by His principles.

Experiencing God's Presence: Faith opens the door to experiencing God's presence and activity in one's life. Through faith, individuals may encounter God in moments of prayer, worship, reflection, and through the workings of His Spirit in their lives.

Growing and Deepening: Faith is a dynamic and evolving aspect of the relationship with God. It grows and deepens through continued engagement, study, prayer, and experience.

In summary, faith serves as the foundation and catalyst for establishing and nurturing a personal relationship with God. It involves trust, surrender, seeking, communication, obedience, and experiencing God's presence, all of which contribute to a deeper and more intimate connection with the divine.

Let's examine some verses that directly approach the development of a personal relationship with God through faith:

Psalm 9:10

"Those who know your name trust in you, for you, LORD, have never forsaken those who seek you."

Psalm 9:10 encourages believers to trust in God based on their knowledge of His character and past faithfulness. The verse underscores the idea that an authentic relationship with God, characterized by seeking Him and knowing Him intimately, leads to a profound and unwavering trust in His reliability. This trust is founded on the assurance that God has consistently been faithful to those who sincerely seek Him.

"Those who know your name trust in you," – this goes beyond an intellectual understanding. It implies a deep, personal relationship with God and an intimate knowledge of His character, attributes, and faithfulness.

"…for you, Lord, have never forsaken those who seek you." – God has unchanging faithfulness and is portrayed as a dependable and constant source of refuge for those who earnestly seek Him.

Mark 11:24

"Therefore I tell you, whatever you ask for in prayer, believe that you have received it, and it will be yours."

Mark 11:24 teaches about the importance of combining prayer with faith. It encourages believers to approach God confidently in prayer, trusting that He can answer according to His wisdom and purposes. The verse underscores the transformative power of faith in the efficacy of prayer, emphasizing the connection between belief and the realization of God's promises.

"Therefore I tell you, whatever you ask for in prayer," - God is approachable. He wants to talk to you and me. We just need to give Him the time He deserves.

"*...believe that you have received it,*" – trusting in God's ability and willingness to answer prayers according to His will.

"*...and it will be yours.*" – Jesus affirms the connection between faith and the realization of the requested outcome. When believers pray with genuine faith and trust, Jesus assures that what they ask for will be granted with the caveat that it will be granted when Jesus feels we are ready – on His time, not ours.

Galatians 2:20

"I have been crucified with Christ and I no longer live, but Christ lives in me. The life I now live in the body, I live by faith in the Son of God, who loved me and gave himself for me."

Galatians 2:20 captures the essence of the believer's identity and relationship with Christ. It conveys the idea of dying to the old self, being spiritually reborn, and living a new life in Christ through faith. This verse is foundational to understanding the transformative power of the gospel in shaping the identity and conduct of a Christian.

"I have been crucified with Christ" – this symbolizes a spiritual death to sin and the old self.

"…and I no longer live," - a radical transformation occurs in the life of a believer. The believer is no longer controlled by the power of sin.

"…but Christ lives in me." - this is the core of the Christian identity as evidenced in the indwelling presence of Christ in the believer. This signifies a union with Christ, where His life becomes the driving force within the believer.

"The life I now live in the body, I live by faith in the Son of God," - the Christian life is characterized by an ongoing trust and reliance on Jesus Christ. Believers recognize Jesus's lordship and rely on His grace and guidance.

"…who loved me and gave himself for me." – the motivation for this transformed life is rooted in the love of Christ. His sacrificial death on the cross is the expression of His love, and believers respond by living in gratitude and devotion.

In summary, faith serves as the foundation and catalyst for establishing and nurturing a personal relationship with God. It involves trust, surrender, seeking, communication, obedience, and experiencing God's presence, all of which contribute to a deeper and more intimate connection with Him.

Meditation: in the spaces provided write down your thoughts and responses to these verses and summarize how faith can help you become more intimate with God and foster a more personal relationship with Him.

____

____

____

____

____

Chapter 5: Conclusion

Walking in faith with Christ means living in a manner that reflects belief in Him as Lord and Savior, and actively following His teachings and example. Here's a summary of what it means:

Trust and Surrender: It involves placing trust in Christ's guidance and surrendering one's will to His purpose, acknowledging His sovereignty over one's life.

Obeying His Teachings: Walking in faith means obeying Christ's commandments and teachings, as outlined in the Bible, and aligning one's actions with His principles of love, compassion, and righteousness.

Dependence on His Strength: It involves relying on Christ's strength and grace to overcome challenges and live a life that honors Him, recognizing one's own limitations and the need for His empowerment.

Following His Example: Walking in faith with Christ entails emulating His example of humility, service, and sacrificial love towards others, seeking to live as He lived and love as He loved.

Fellowship and Prayer: It involves cultivating a close relationship with Christ through regular prayer, worship, and fellowship with other believers, allowing His presence to guide and shape one's life.

Perseverance and Endurance: Walking in faith requires perseverance and endurance through trials and difficulties, trusting in Christ's faithfulness and promises even amid adversity.

Growth and Transformation: It entails continual growth and transformation as one's faith deepens and matures, leading to a life that increasingly reflects Christlikeness and bears fruit for His kingdom.

In essence, walking in faith with Christ is a journey of discipleship characterized by trust, obedience, dependence, fellowship, perseverance, and transformation, as believers seek to live out their commitment to follow Him in every aspect of their lives.

Feel free to note any additional feelings, comments, and/or sentiments regarding this first book of this series:

____

____

____

____

____

____

____

____

____

____

____